Copyrighted Material

The Pre & Post College Student Pocket Guide
to Success
Copyright © 2017 by Renee J. Bey

ALL RIGHTS RESERVED

No part of this publication may be
reproduced, stored in a retrieval system or
transmitted, in any form or by any means –
electronic, mechanical, photocopying,
recording or otherwise without prior written
permission, except for the inclusion of brief
quotations in a review.

For information about this title or to order
other books and or electronic media, contact
the Publisher:

Unspoken Knowledge Publishing, LLC
P.O. Box 3
New Boston, MI 48164
www.unspokenknowledge.com
books@unspokenknowledge.com

ISBN: 978-0-9986895-0-0
Printed in the United States of America
Cover Design by: Joanna Darby

Dedication

I dedicate this book to my husband Antonio Bey for his love and support and to my two beautiful and intelligent daughters AnTonia and Anaiah Bey, who have encouraged and motivated me to earn my Bachelor's and Master's Degree and for always having faith in me that I can achieve whatever I set my mind to.

I dedicate this book to my sister Joanna Darby who has always strongly encouraged and supported me in all my passions and endeavors including the writing of this book.

I dedicate this book to my sister-n-law Leta Bey who has encouraged me to write a book.

Table of Contents

PREFACE 1

CHAPTER 1 6

Rules of the Road to Avoiding College Debt 6

Getting Involved in Extracurricular Activities 9

ACT and SAT Exam 14

SAT vs. ACT: Understanding the Differences 16

When should you take the ACT and SAT Exam? ... 19

Scholarships 24

Federal Pell Grant 27

How to pay for college when you don't have a scholarship or financial aid? 30

Career Choice 38

Chapter 1 Key Takeaways 43

CHAPTER 2 47

How to avoid late payments, bad credit & the lack of credit 47

Ways to budget your money wisely 51

The 3 Credit Bureaus 53

Chapter 2 Key Takeaways 60

CHAPTER 3 62

Preparing for the Workforce 62

Internship 63

Network 66

College Alumni Association 67

Chapter 3 Key Takeaways 68

CHAPTER 4 70

Saving Early for Retirement 70

401k, 403b, & 457b Plan 72

Traditional & Roth IRA 76

Money Market Savings Account 77

Applying Merit Increases to your 401k, 403b, & 457b Plan 79

Chapter 4 Key Takeaways 81

CONCLUSION 83

REFERENCES 85

RESOURCES 87

PREFACE

It has been my desire for quite some time to inform high school and college students about the rules of the road to success prior to attending college, during college, and after college. In this college student pocket guide, I will be focusing on how to avoid college debt, late payments, having bad credit and the lack of credit.

I will also discuss several ways in how to prepare for the workforce and the importance of saving early for retirement. Furthermore, I want to inspire those who feel that there aren't any affordable options to attend college that there *are* options. In addition, I want to change the mindset of those who feel that attending college will only bury them in debt. I now have an opportunity to share my wisdom regarding these important topics.

I can honestly say that I am college debt free! However, I didn't have the necessary resources and the thorough knowledge of applying for scholarships when I was in high school. So, I initially attended Wayne County Community College, and with the help of receiving a Federal Pell grant to fund my education, I earned my Associate's Degree in Pre- Social Work. I took a break in attending school because I was indecisive in my career choice. I really just didn't know for sure what I wanted to do. I had a desire to help others, but I didn't think Social Work was the best career choice for me at that time.

During my educational break, I had two beautiful daughters who inspired and motivated me to want more out of life and to receive a higher education. I started working at a bank and became interested in the banking industry. I was blessed with obtaining a banking position that offered tuition reimbursement. So, I jumped on that opportunity and enrolled in Wayne State University and earned my Bachelor's Degree in Finance. I took a brief break from school. After deciding that I really wanted to pursue my Master's Degree and still having the opportunity to participate in the bank tuition reimbursement program, I attended Walsh College of Accountancy and Business and earned my Masters of Science Degree in Management. Juggling between school, work, and family life was challenging and required motivation, determination, dedication and perseverance.

You can do whatever you set your mind to do. Please, don't let anyone or anything stop you from your own success and what you are destined to be.

CHAPTER 1

Rules of the Road to Avoiding College Debt

How often have you heard someone say they are thousands of dollars in debt after graduating from college? Too many times, right? You wonder how someone can be in so much debt after graduating from college. Furthermore, it discourages you from even wanting to attend college. Well, don't worry. There are several ways in which you can attend college and avoid being in debt. First, I wanted to inform you about some of the common mistakes that college students make prior to attending college that could ultimately hurt their chances of avoiding college debt in the future. The following is a list of mistakes high school students make.

1. They have not been involved in any extracurricular activities or leadership programs within or outside of the high school they attend, which makes it difficult

to become highly considered as a scholarship recipient. Nowadays, good grades are just not good enough.

2. They do not prep for the ACT and SAT exam, which can diminish a high school student's chance from scoring high on the ACT and SAT exam.

3. They do not take the time to search for scholarships to apply for college.

4. They search for scholarships, but never take the time to apply for college scholarships.

5. They do not apply for Pell grants.

6. They are indecisive about their career choice.

Getting Involved in Extracurricular Activities

Let me start by discussing the importance of getting involved in school activities and those activities outside of school. Even though University and College scholarship recipient criteria involve the GPA (Grade Point Average), ACT and SAT scores, and financial need, many scholarship donors seek scholarship recipients that have been involved in extracurricular activities or have a unique talent or circumstance. They are looking for someone who is able to receive good grades as well as be involved in activities; whether the activities are in school or outside of school. They are looking for someone with drive, motivation, determination, perseverance, as well as multi-tasking and leadership skills. A high GPA demonstrates a portion of that. Most colleges and universities require the scholarship applicants to have earned at least a 3.0 G.P. A., However, strive to obtain and maintain a 3.3 G.P.A or higher, as this will better your chances to receive an academic scholarship.

When completing the university or college scholarship application, a student must fill out the FAFSA (Free Application for Student Aid) form, so that their financial need is determined. For those students whose parents income may affect the eligibility requirements in order to receive financial aid, taking the time to create a portfolio of your accomplishments (which occurred in school and/or outside of school) during your high school years can tremendously help in obtaining a donor scholarship from organizations that award scholarships based on a student's involvement in community service, race, religion, unique talents and circumstances. Following is a list of some school activities that are great to get involved in.

1. Athletics
2. National Honor Society
3. Student Council
4. Business Club
5. Performing Arts/Band Club

The following is a list of some activities to get involved in outside of school.

1. Community Service
2. Youth Leadership Program
3. Dance Program
4. Band/Music
5. Boys and Girls Club
6. Athletics
7. Girls & Boys Scout

ACT and SAT Exam

In regards to the ACT and SAT exam, it is imperative to prep for the ACT and SAT starting as early as freshman year of high school or sooner if possible, so that you have the best possible chance to earn a high score, which will offer you a greater opportunity to receive a scholarship and attend that university that you have been dreaming of attending ever since you were a child. You may be asking yourself what these exams consist of. The ACT is a nationally administered, standardized test that helps colleges to evaluate candidates. The ACT exam consists of four sections which include English, Mathematics, Reading, & Science. The exam lasts between 2 hours and 55 minutes to 3 hours and 40 minutes depending if the writing test is included. The SAT is a scholastic aptitude test to measure candidates' aptitude and mental ability. The SAT exam consists of three sections which include Reading, Writing & Language and Math. The exam lasts between 3 hours to 3 hours and 50 minutes depending if the essay is included.

You may be wondering what the difference between the two exams are, so let me explain.

SAT vs. ACT: Understanding the Differences

In terms of understanding the differences between the SAT and the ACT, there isn't a significant difference in content between the two; however the ACT has a science testing section and the SAT does not. In addition, the SAT has a math section in which a calculator can't be used. The testing for the ACT math section is slightly more complex than the SAT math section. So, your math comfort level may help you determine which exam fits you best. The SAT exam provides students more time when taking an exam. If you find yourself needing more time when taking an exam, you may want to consider the SAT exam.

Some colleges may be more interested in one exam over the other, so please contact the colleges that you are interested in to see which exam may be more favorable for that particular college.

Please keep in mind that you can take both the ACT & the SAT if you like.

Even though there is an option for the writing portion of the ACT & SAT exam, it is in your best interest to take the writing portion of the exam, as most colleges are interested in seeing how well a student comprehends the material and convey his or her thoughts.

Extensively prep for the ACT and SAT Exam at least 2 – 3 months in advance of the Exam date. ACT and Kaplan have partnered up to provide live and engaging instruction at a reasonable and affordable cost, and free for low-income students. Please reach out to your school counselor or advisor and ask about the eligibility requirements for receiving ACT and SAT free waivers to take the ACT and SAT at no charge.

When should you take the ACT and SAT Exam?

The ideal time to take the ACT and SAT exam is during the spring of junior year of high school. That way you have enough time to re-take the exam if you choose to do so in the fall of your senior year of high school. *It is a must to keep in mind the college and scholarship admissions deadline when making your exam decisions.* When submitting both the college and scholarship application, you must also submit your ACT or SAT scores or both along with the applications. According to Kaplan.com, the following are the rankings for the ACT & SAT scores.

Regarding the ACT exam, the composite score is the average of all test scores rounded to the nearest whole number.

ACT is scored on a 1-36 scale.

The following are the rankings of the ACT scores.

Ranking of Scores	Composite
Top	28-36
Competitive	24-27
Above Average	20-26
Below Average	19

The following SAT ranking of scores is scored on a 1600-point scale, scored between 200 and 800.

The following are the rankings of the SAT Evidence Based Reading and Writing scores.

Ranking of Scores	Reading & Writing
Top	660-800
Competitive	590-650
Above Average	510-580
Below Average	500 or Lower

The following are the rankings of the SAT Math scores.

Ranking of Scores	Math
Top	680-800
Competitive	610-670
Above Average	520-600
Below Average	510 or Lower

The composite score on the SAT is the sum of the Math score & the Reading and Writing score. The following are the SAT composite scores.

Ranking of Scores	Composite
Top	1340 - 1600
Competitive	1200 - 1320
Above Average	1030 - 1180
Below Average	1010 - 400

Please visit the following websites to obtain the most current ACT & SAT rankings, as they are subject to change.

https://www.kaptest.com/act/whats-a-good-act-score

https://www.kaptest.com/sat/whats-a-good-sat-score

Please refer to the following websites for more information regarding the ACT & SAT free practice tests.

http://www.act.org/

https://www.collegeboard.org/

https://kaplan.com/

Scholarships

Now that I have discussed the importance of students' being involved in extracurricular activities, leadership programs and prepping for the ACT and SAT exam, I would like to discuss scholarships in more detail and when high school students should start applying for scholarships.

A scholarship is an award of financial aid that is awarded to a student to further his or her education. Receiving a scholarship is based on certain criteria and the money is not required to be repaid. It is imperative to be motivated and to take the initiative to seek and also apply for scholarships that meet your eligibility requirements.

You can start applying for scholarships as early as freshman year of high school for scholarships offered by donors; however applying for scholarships for universities and colleges typically starts senior year of high school. Please take the initiative and begin the scholarship search to colleges at least in your junior year of high school.

Please understand that you can still receive academic scholarships; however you have a far better chance of obtaining a donor scholarship if you can offer more than good grades.

The following are website links that provides scholarship options.

https://www.fastweb.com/
https://www.scholarships.com/
http://www.college-financial-aid-advice.com/scholarship-money-for-college.html

Federal Pell Grant

Many high school graduates do not take advantage of the Federal Pell Grant. This is free money that doesn't have to be repaid, unless under certain circumstances. According to fafsa.gov, the Pell Grant can be awarded for no more than twelve semesters. The maximum amount that a student can receive yearly for the period of July 1, 2017 thru June 30, 2018 and July 1, 2018 through June 30, 2019 is $5,920.00. The amount awarded to the student depends on the following:

1. Financial need
2. Cost of attendance
3. Status as a full time or part time student
4. Plans to attend school for a full academic year or less

The following are some circumstances in which the Federal Pell Grant may have to be repaid.

1. A student's early withdrawal from the program for which the grant was given to the student.

2. The student enrollment status has changed that reduced his or her eligibility for a grant.

3. The student received outside grants or scholarships that have reduced his or her need for federal student aid.

Please refer to the FAFSA and Student Aid website for more information on Pell Grants.

https://fafsa.gov/

https://studentaid.ed.gov/sa/

How to pay for college when you don't have a scholarship or financial aid?

For those who have read the common high school mistakes and have said to themselves, "I've done all those steps and still didn't receive a scholarship, a desired scholarship award amount, or the financial aid that I was seeking", please don't give up or be discouraged. There are ways that you can still attend college and avoid being in college debt after graduation.

Below is a list of ways in which you can attend college and not be burdened with excessive college debt.

1. Attend a community college for the first two years and then work on receiving a scholarship to a university. Traditionally, community colleges are far more inexpensive and affordable than universities. NOTE: It is very important to speak with a counselor at the community college of your choice to see if the credits that you take there are transferrable to the University

that you plan to attend once you have graduated from that community college. If the credits do not transfer to the University that you desire and plan on attending, this can be very disappointing and will have you spending more money and time taking more courses at the desired University or you may feel forced to attend a University not of your choice that accepts the community college credits.

2. Apply for jobs where tuition reimbursement or assistance is available. It is best to apply for

jobs that are in the field that you are majoring in. By obtaining a job that you are majoring in, will give you the work experience in your field prior to you graduating from college. Work experience is a plus, as many employers look for someone with one or more years of experience when applying for a position. When utilizing tuition reimbursement, the best way to fund your education is to apply for one credit card with a limit that doesn't exceed the amount you need to pay off your classes and to purchase textbooks each semester. If you do not receive the desired credit card limit that you need for the number of classes that you would like to be enrolled in each semester, I recommend only taking the number of classes that the credit card limit will cover. Once that semester is over and you have received a grade that meets the requirements, (which is usually a C or better), you will need to submit your grades to the employer to obtain the tuition reimbursement check. When you receive the reimbursement check, pay off your credit card in full.

DO NOT SPEND THAT MONEY ON ANYTHING ELSE as this is how the debt snowball occurs and you will begin to fall deeper and deeper in debt.

3. Apply for the federal work-study program at the college you are attending. The program provides part-time jobs for undergraduate as well as graduate students with a financial need. Please refer to the following link for more information regarding work-study programs.

https://studentaid.ed.gov/sa/types/work-study

4. I really don't recommend student loans, but if you have to obtain a student loan, get a loan that you can pay back in a fairly reasonable amount of time. ONLY TAKE A LOAN FOR THE AMOUNT THAT YOU NEED! It will only take longer and become more difficult to repay the loan, when taking out more than what is absolutely needed. Do not wait until the loan goes into forbearance; whereas payments on your student loan are temporarily not being paid, but interest on the loan is still being accrued. Make monthly

payments on the loan, so that it is being reduced while you are attending college.

Career Choice

Identifying what interest you career wise and being proactive in researching the variety of career fields, while still attending high school can save you money and time in the future. Many high school students are initially indecisive about what career they want to pursue. I get it. That was me in high school and college. To play it somewhat safe, many will take general classes or take a break from school, until they figure out what they really want to do in life. This wastes a tremendous amount of time and/or money. Keep in mind that you are attending college to have a career and not a job, so really think of a career choice that you see yourself doing long term. The Bureau of Labor Statistics website, https://www.bls.gov/, provides detailed information for occupations. In order to locate and find detailed information regarding the occupation that interests you, click on the tab named "Publications" on the homepage and then select the Publication link "Occupational Outlook Handbook" For ex., if you are interested in a career in

Finance as a Financial Analyst, under the tab named "Occupation Groups" you would select the "Business and Financial" link. This link will take you to all business and financial occupations which also includes the Financial Analyst. Once you click on the Financial Analyst link, it will provide detailed information such as the median pay, the typical entry-level education, the job outlook, what a Financial Analyst does, the work environment and similar occupations to name a few. While reviewing the occupations on the Bureau of Labor Statistics website below, please review

and be mindful of the following list of factors to consider when deciding your career choice.
https://www.bls.gov/

1. What does the position entail?
2. What level of passion do you have for the career field?
3. How important is work life balance for you and does that career offer it?
4. Will you be content with the salary?
5. Is the career field in high demand?

In addition to the Bureau of Labor Statistics website, I would suggest that you take a career test to find out what career may best fit your personality.

The following is a link to a free career test website.

https://www.123test.com/career-test/

Chapter 1 Key Takeaways

Remember the importance of getting involved in extracurricular activities. Keep in mind that parents income is typically factored in when determining the students financial need when applying for FAFSA. Parents that earn a higher income could negatively affect a student chance of receiving financial aid. So, it is very important to create a portfolio of your accomplishments as this can greatly increase your chances of being awarded a donor scholarship. In many instances, good grades are not good enough anymore when being highly considered for a scholarship, especially donor scholarships.

Prepping for the ACT and SAT is a must in order for you to better your chances of earning a top or competitive score. Searching for scholarships and actually applying for them as well as Federal Pell grants can allow you to have a free ride or pay very little to attend college. In addition, researching and selecting the career field that best fits you can save you money and time in the future.

All of these necessary steps will greatly prepare you to graduate from college with little to no debt. Even if you didn't obtain a scholarship or financial aid, tuition reimbursement is an awesome opportunity to take advantage of. Please remember to use the credit card to initially pay for your classes and then pay the credit card off as soon as you receive the tuition reimbursement check from your employer. Do not spend the tuition reimbursement check on anything else, as this will cause the accumulation of debt.

Please have and keep that "can do" attitude. You can live a less stressful life and be able to do the things you long to do in life more comfortably without having to be worried, concerned, and burdened about drowning in debt.

Be Inspired!

CHAPTER 2

How to avoid late payments, bad credit & the lack of credit

Have you ever heard anyone say that their credit is ruined or that no one will give them a chance to purchase a car or house because they don't have credit and the only way they can get one is if someone cosigns for them? Well, you can avoid this from happening to you, if you avoid some common mistakes.

Below are some common mistakes many college students make that can ultimately hurt them in the future.

1. They don't budget their money wisely.
2. They constantly pay their bills late.
3. They haven't built any credit for the three credit bureaus to report.

First, I would like to discuss the importance of budgeting and the setbacks you may encounter when you don't budget your money and are constantly paying your bills late. As a college student, you must be responsible and proactive. Many college students are spending money on everything except for what is a necessity. Think about what you are spending your money on and ask yourself, "Is this something I need or want"?

Many college students are renting apartments or have leased or bought a vehicle; however they are late on paying their monthly rent, utility bills, or car payment because they have spent their money on something that wasn't needed or within their budget.

Each time you are late on your monthly payment; it works against you in the credit world. The late payment will be reported on your credit report. Each late inquiry you receive on your credit report decreases your credit score with the 3 credit bureaus as well as decreases your chance of obtaining a decent interest rate when making a purchase in the future, whether it is a house, car, or etc.

Ways to budget your money wisely

1. Strive to purchase groceries and prepare your meals whenever possible to avoid spending your money at fast food restaurants. Cook meals that will last a few days. This will help you save money and eat healthier.

2. Whenever possible, instead of purchasing brand new textbooks, purchase used textbooks.

3. Minimize the amount of purchases you charge on your credit card. Only charge what you can pay off within a reasonable amount of time.

4. Create or download a free budget worksheet to keep track of what you spend as this will help you identify what expenses you need to cut back on to stay within your budget.

5. Lastly, if you don't need it, don't buy it.

The 3 Credit Bureaus

There are 3 national credit bureaus which consist of Equifax, Experian, & Transunion. They are the 3 major credit reporting agencies. They all collect, update, and store credit history on the majority of US consumers. They are similar; however data may be captured and stored differently by each one. They all provide FICO scores. The FICO score is a credit scoring system developed by the Fair Isaac Corporation to help determine a person's credit worthiness. The credit score is a number that is used to predict how likely a person will pay their loan back on time. According to the following website, https://www.myfico.com/credit-education/whats-in-your-credit-score/, there are 5 main factors that affect your credit score.

1. Payment History (35% of FICO score)
2. Debt/amounts owed (30% of FICO score)
3. Age of credit history (15%)
4. New credit/Inquiries (10%)
5. Mix of accounts/type of credit (10%)

The credit score ranges from 300 – 850. The higher the number, the less risk you represent to the lender or insurer. Those with a score of 760 or higher are more likely to get the best rates when they borrow. You should check your credit score and credit report once a year to make sure that all the information on the credit report is accurate. If you find that your report has inaccurate information, please reach out to that specific credit bureau that has the misinformation and dispute the inaccuracies.

Please refer to the following websites for more information on FICO scores.

http://www.myfico.com/

https://www.consumerfinance.gov/ask-cfpb/what-is-a-fico-score-en-1883/

No credit is just as bad as or worse than poor credit. You are probably asking yourself how no credit is just as bad as or worse than poor credit. Well, without having any credit, lenders and insurers can't refer to your credit history to see how well you have been paying your bills. It doesn't give them much to work with if you don't have any history on how timely you pay your bills. More than likely, you will either be turned down on getting a loan or you will receive a higher interest rate because the lenders or insurers are taking a risk on providing you a loan or insuring you because they are unsure of how credible and responsible you are when making payments. To avoid receiving a high interest rate or being turned down for a loan, it is highly recommended to build your credit history early. You can build a good credit history promptly by applying for and obtaining ONE credit card. A small limit of no more than $200 is all you should need to build your credit. Charge a very minimal amount each month that is within your budget and then pay the debt off in its entirety within 30 days of the charge so that you are building credit promptly and demonstrating that you are paying your bills off on time. If you can't pay the debt off in its entirety within the 30 days, at least pay the minimum amount due on time. Please keep in mind when charging expenses on your credit card, it is recommended to keep your total credit utilization rate/ratio below 30% as it is considered an indicator that you're doing a good job of being responsible and managing your credit because you're far from overspending. A higher rate, however, could be a flag to potential lenders or creditors that you're having trouble managing your finances. The utilization rate/ratio is the amount of revolving credit you're currently using divided by the total amount of revolving credit you have available. It is how much you currently owe divided by your credit limit.

Chapter 2 Key Takeaways

Now that you have been armed with the knowledge of how important it is to pay your bills on time to avoid bad credit and knowing that having some credit is far better than having no credit at all, you have the opportunity to obtain better interest rates that will save you money in the long run. The higher your interest rates are, the higher your monthly car, mortgage, and any other loan payments will be. Purchase groceries and cook meals that will last a few days instead of purchasing fast food. When possible, purchase used textbooks instead of new textbooks. Minimize your credit card charges and pay them off each month or at least the minimum amount within 30 days and remember to maintain a utilization rate/ratio below 30% for your credit charges so that it indicates good credit managing. Download a free budget worksheet or create one yourself to keep track of your expenses and to identify what you need to cut back on. If you don't need it, don't buy it.

Budget & pay your bills on time!

CHAPTER 3

Preparing for the Workforce

Some college students have a difficult time finding a job after graduation and have become very discouraged about their future. To avoid this from happening, there are three options that college students should highly consider. They are as follows.

1. Internship
2. Network (Family & Friends)
3. Join your College Alumni Association

Internship

Many employers seek employees that have obtained some experience when applying for a position. Unfortunately, many college students do not have work experience in their field of study after graduating from college. It would be in your best interest to have an internship prior to your college graduation. This way you are not only armed with education in your field of study, but you will also have an opportunity to have gained some work experience in your field of study. Internships are offered by an employer to a potential employee. Internships offer students experiences in the industry related to their field of study for a certain period of time. Internships can last from one month to 12 months. Typically, internships last about 10 to 12 weeks. Begin your search for internships in your field early and apply for several internships, so that you have a better opportunity of receiving one.

After completing your internship, there is a great chance that the company will offer you a position upon graduation, if you have done an exceptional job as an intern. Internships can be paid or unpaid. It depends on the industry.

Network

Reach out to family and friends to find out if someone is hiring in your field of study. You never know who they may know. Many times employers hire family and friends of someone already working in their company. So, it never hurts to reach out and inquire.

Linkedin.com is also a great way to network and to showcase your skills. If you don't have work experience to include in your Linkedin.com profile, you can still add your educational background because there are some employers who hire those who don't have any experience at all.

College Alumni Association

Make sure to join your college alumni association. This can help you currently and years later in receiving career planning and placement guidance and assistance.

Chapter 3 Key Takeaways

Please stay mindful of preparing for the workforce while you are attending college. If you don't already have a position that relates to your field of study, it is imperative to receive an internship so that you have some work experience in your field of study prior to graduation.

The more work experience you have will better your chances of getting a job shortly after graduation. Network with as many people as you can. Start with family and friends. They can take you a long way with finding a job.

Take advantage of Linkedin.com. This website will help you to showcase your educational skills as well as your work experience. Join your college alumni association. This association not only helps you now, but it can help you years down the road with your career planning and job placement.

Be Proactive and Communicate!

CHAPTER 4

Saving Early for Retirement

We all work to have a place to live, eat, pay our bills, drive a car, and provide for our family. We also work now to be able to retire comfortably later in life and continue to live the way we have been living. Unfortunately, many individuals who have been working for quite some time do not have an adequate amount of savings to retire by their retirement age. The retirement age is 67 for those born after 1959. Please refer to the Social security website below for more information on retirement.

www.SSA.gov

There are several ways in which you can start saving for retirement early in your career so that you can be very prepared for when you decide to retire. You want to start saving in your early 20's. The following are some ways to save for retirement.

1. Participate in your employer sponsored retirement savings plan (401k, 403b, & 457b plan)
2. Participate in a Traditional or Roth IRA
3. Open a Money Market Savings Account
4. Apply a portion or the entire merit increases to your employer sponsored retirement plan.

401k, 403b, & 457b Plan

When you begin your career, one of the most important benefits you want to make sure your employer offers is a retirement plan. 401k, 403b, and 457b plans are all offered retirement savings plans provided by the employer. The savings plans will consist of investments that usually involve stock, bonds, and money market investments. The significant difference between the 401k, 403b, and 457b retirement plan is who the plan is offered by. The 401k plan is offered by for-profit organizations. The 403b retirement plan is offered by non-profit organizations and the 457b plan is offered by a tax-exempt organization or the state and local government.

The most lucrative retirement plan offered by an employer is a company match contribution plan. For example, a company can match 100% of what you contribute to the retirement plan up to 5% of your base salary.

Employees are able to invest and save part of their earnings before taxes are taken out. The taxes aren't paid until the money is withdrawn. An employee must reach the vested period, prior to being able to withdraw any company match contributions. The typical timeframe to be vested ranges from 3 to 5 years. However, keep in mind that there are penalties to withdrawing funds from your 401k early. Many employees are selecting the target date funds. They are becoming very popular because it involves a combination of stocks and bonds that has a lower risk and becomes more conservative as you reach retirement. As of 2018, the annual contribution limit for the 401k plan is $18,500.00 with a catch up contribution of $6,000.00 which begins at the age of 50. For more information on 401k, 403b, 457b, please refer to www.irs.gov.

Traditional & Roth IRA

The Traditional and Roth IRA are not sponsored by the employer. This is not an investment plan that is automatically enrolled. The account owner will make contributions and select investment options of his or her choice.

Currently in 2018, the annual contribution limit for both the Roth and Traditional IRA is $5,500 and $6,500 for those ages 50 and older. Please refer to www.irs.gov for more information on Roth & Traditional IRA.

Money Market Savings Account

In addition to the 401k, 403b, or the 457b plan and the IRA plan, if you are looking to save money even faster, set aside $100 or more a month to deposit into your savings account. The Money Market Savings account is a type of savings account that usually earns more interest than a basic savings account and there are no penalties to withdraw funds from the account. To open up a Money Market

Savings account, the minimum deposit and balance is typically higher than the basic savings account. The minimum amount to open up this type of an account is usually $500 or more.

The interest can be compounded daily or monthly and usually paid monthly. There is a limit on the number of times you transfer and withdraw. Usually, you can't have more than six transfers or withdrawals during each monthly period. You can deposit money into the Money Market Account via Online Banking, direct deposit, check, or physically walking into the bank and providing cash. For more information please call or visit your local Credit Union or Banking Institution.

Applying Merit Increases to your 401k, 403b, & 457b Plan

A merit increase is a raise or increase in pay provided by your employer. Managers will rate the employees, usually based on their performance over the last year. The amount of the increase an employee receives depends on the employee's rated level of performance over the last year.

If you are looking to save more money, each time you receive a merit increase, add a portion or the entire merit increase to your 401k, 403b, or 457b plan. The more you earn the more you are taxed, so it's not a bad idea to add at least a portion of your merit increase in your employer retirement plan.

Chapter 4 Key Takeaways

Please be aware and concerned about how you are going to live comfortably and survive in your later years. It is in your best interest to start saving in your early 20's, so that you have a substantial amount of savings by the time your retirement age approaches.

The 401k, 403b, & 457b plan are great savings plan that you can take advantage of through your employer. You can also take advantage of savings investments through the Traditional or

Roth IRA, as well as make additional deposits into a Money Market savings account. Applying a portion or your entire merit increases to your 401k, 403b, or 457b plan will allow your retirement savings to grow even faster.

Don't wait until it's too late, start saving today!

CONCLUSION

Your life and the way you live it is everything. The outcome of your life is due to the choices you made along the way in life. Stand up and have the desire to be somebody special it won't take much because you already are somebody special.

Everyone has some type of struggle or obstacle to overcome when trying to get where they want to be in life, but everyone can make it to their destination if they choose to. Through focus, perseverance, determination, and the will to be successful, it will happen. Please take heed to "The Pre & Post College Student Pocket Guide to Success" because it will take you far and places you never even dreamed of.

REFERENCES

Retrieved from: https://www.kaptest.com/act/whats-a-good-act-score

Retrieved from: https://www.kaptest.com/sat/whats-a-good-sat-score

Retrieved from: https://www.ssa.gov/planners/retire/1960.html

Retrieved from: https://www.myfico.com/credit-education/whats-in-your-credit-score/

Retrieved from: https://www.consumerfinance.gov/ask-cfpb/what-is-a-fico-score-en-1883/

Retrieved from: https://www.experian.com/blogs/ask-experian/credit-education/score-basics/credit-utilization-rate/

Retrieved from: https://www.princetonreview.com/college/sat-act

Retrieved from: https://studentaid.ed.gov/sa/types/work-study

Retrieved from: https://studentaid.ed.gov/sa/types/grants-scholarships/pell#how-much-money

Retrieved from: https://www.irs.gov/retirement-plans/plan-participant-employee/retirement-topics-401k-and-profit-sharing-plan-contribution-limits

Retrieved from: https://www.irs.gov/retirement-plans/plan-participant-employee/retirement-topics-catch-up-contributions

Retrieved from: https://www.irs.gov/retirement-plans/plan-participant-employee/retirement-topics-ira-contribution-limits

RESOURCES

http://www.act.org/

https://www.collegeboard.org/

https://fafsa.gov/

https://studentaid.ed.gov/sa/

https://www.bls.gov/

www.SSA.gov

www.irs.gov

http://www.myfico.com/

https://www.experian.com/

https://www.equifax.com/personal/

https://www.transunion.com/

www.Linkedin.com

https://www.fastweb.com

https://www.scholarships.com/

https://profileonline.collegeboard.com

https://www.123test.com/career-test/

http://www.college-financial-aid-advice.com/scholarship-money-for-college.html

http://www.internships.com/student

http://www.internships.com/employer/resources/setup/duration

www.ingramcontent.com/pod-product-compliance
Lightning Source LLC
Chambersburg PA
CBHW050442010526
44118CB00013B/1646